North Dakota
The Peace Garden State

Marcia Amidon Lusted

PowerKiDS press™

New York

Published in 2011 by The Rosen Publishing Group, Inc.
29 East 21st Street, New York, NY 10010

First Edition

Editor: Maggie Murphy
Book Design: Greg Tucker
Photo Researcher: Jessica Gerweck

Photo Credits: Cover Michael Melford/Getty Images; p. 5 Annie Griffiths/National Geographic/Getty Images; p. 7 MPI/Getty Images; pp. 9, 11, 17, 22 (flag, flower) Shutterstock.com; p. 13 Phil Schermeister/Getty Images; p. 15 VisionsofAmerica/Joe Sohm/Getty Images; p. 19 © Rabouan Jean-Baptiste/age fotostock; p. 22 (tree) © www.iStockphoto.com/Larry Burditt; p. 22 (fish) © www.iStockphoto.com/Krzysztof Odziomek; p. 22 (bird) © www.iStockphoto.com/Stephen Muskie; p. 22 (Peggy Lee) Michael Ochs Archives/Getty Images; p. 22 (Josh Duhamel) Frazer Harrison/Getty Images; p. 22 (Kellen Lutz) Soul Brother/FilmMagic/for Good Day New York/Getty Images.

Library of Congress Cataloging-in-Publication Data

Lusted, Marcia Amidon.
  North Dakota : the Peace Garden State / Marcia Amidon Lusted. — 1st ed.
     p. cm. — (Our amazing states)
  Includes index.
  ISBN 978-1-4488-0664-5 (library binding) — ISBN 978-1-4488-0764-2 (pbk.) — ISBN 978-1-4488-0765-9 (6-pack)
  1. North Dakota—Juvenile literature. I. Title.
  F636.3.L87 2011
  978.4—dc22
                              2009054345

Manufactured in the United States of America

CPSIA Compliance Information: Batch #WS10PK: For Further Information contact Rosen Publishing, New York, New York at 1-800-237-9932

Contents

A Land of Peace and Friendship

Where can you see **Scandinavian** festivals, Native American powwows, and cowboys? Early **pioneers** traveled through this place in their covered wagons, and today giant wind **turbines** stand against the open sky. Where are you? You are in North Dakota!

North Dakota is one of the Great Plains states. It sits between Minnesota and Montana and above South Dakota. Its northern border is Canada.

The name Dakota comes from a Sioux word that means "friend" or "ally." North Dakota is also called the Peace Garden State because it is home to the International Peace Garden. This flower garden celebrates the friendship between the United States and Canada.

Here, hot-air balloons fly in the air over Fargo, North Dakota. More people live in Fargo than in any other city in North Dakota.

Explorers and Pioneers

The earliest people to live in North Dakota were Native Americans, such as the Mandans. Later, French **explorers** came looking for furs and claimed the area for France. After the Louisiana Purchase in 1803, President Thomas Jefferson sent Meriwether Lewis and William Clark to explore the land the United States had bought from France. They spent the winter in North Dakota and became friends with the Mandans.

When the Northern Pacific Railroad was built in the 1870s, many pioneers came to North Dakota. About 100,000 more people moved there between 1879 and 1886 to claim free land under Congress's Homestead Act of 1862. On November 2, 1889, North Dakota became the thirty-ninth state.

This painting from 1850 shows women from North Dakota's Mandan people dancing. The Mandan people lived along the Missouri River in present-day North Dakota and South Dakota.

From Rocky Buttes to Flat Prairies

North Dakota has many different kinds of land. Western North Dakota is part of the Great Plains. The badlands are also found in the western part of the state. There you can find rocky buttes, or steep hills with flat tops, and deep **canyons**. Ancient **fossils** and **petrified** wood are also found there.

The eastern part of the state has flat grassy prairies with rich soil for farming. The Red River flows there. The Missouri River winds through the center of the state.

North Dakota's weather can be very cold or very hot. It gets as cold as -60° F (-51° C) and as hot as 100° F (38° C)! However, the state gets only about 25 inches (64 cm) of snow every year.

This is a rocky butte in the badlands of western North Dakota. The word "butte" comes from the French word for "small hill." However, many buttes are very large.

Wildflowers and Wild Horses

Because of its flat plains and rocky hills, North Dakota does not have many kinds of trees. Fir and pine trees grow in hilly areas. Cottonwoods, elms, and quaking aspen grow on the prairies, mainly near rivers. However, North Dakota's prairies have many kinds of wildflowers. Prairie crocus and flax grow in the spring. Black-eyed Susans and prickly-pear cacti grow in the summer, followed by curlycup gumweed and wild prairie roses.

Wild horses called Nokota once ran wild on the prairies. Nokota are now kept safe by the government and by private groups. Ground squirrels live in huge underground **burrows**, and coyotes prowl through the badlands. Bison used to be common but now live only in state parks.

Here, a coyote stands in the snow. *Inset*: The pasqueflower, shown here, is a native wildflower in North Dakota.

What Do People Do in North Dakota?

Farming is a big part of North Dakota's **economy** because of its rich soil. Do you like pasta? Chances are the wheat in your spaghetti was grown in North Dakota. Barley, sunflower seeds, and sugar beets are also grown there. Ranchers raise cattle for beef, cows for milk, and hogs. Many farmers also raise turkeys.

Mining is also important in North Dakota. Petroleum, coal, and natural gas come from the ground. Huge **refineries** turn coal into a kind of natural gas, which travels to other states through big pipelines. Because North Dakota is so windy, companies are also using wind turbines to create electricity.

This boy is learning how to be a cowboy on a ranch in Grassy Butte, North Dakota. He is holding a lasso, or a piece of rope used to catch loose animals.

Visiting Bismarck

North Dakota's capital is Bismarck, in the south central part of the state. The state capitol is called the Skyscraper on the Prairie because it is 19 stories tall! The grassy lawn in front of the building is called the Capitol Mall. In 2007, almost 9,000 people gathered there and set a new world record for making the most snow angels in one place at one time!

There are many interesting things to do in Bismarck. Fort Abraham Lincoln State Park and Camp Hancock teach visitors about pioneer history. At the On-a-Slant Village, you can see where the Mandan tribe built earth lodges, or homes made from willow branches, grass, and earth.

This statue of Sacagawea, a Shoshone Native American who traveled with Lewis and Clark, stands in front of the North Dakota Heritage Center, in Bismarck.

Roosevelt's North Dakota

Theodore Roosevelt went to North Dakota to hunt bison in 1883. He decided he wanted to become a cattle rancher and bought two ranches there. Later, Roosevelt said, "I never would have been president if it had not been for my experiences in North Dakota." Today, parts of his ranches are included in the Theodore Roosevelt National Park.

The park is located in the badlands. It includes places such as Peaceful Valley, where visitors can ride horses on trails. At the Painted Canyon Overlook, there are beautiful views of the badlands.

Visitors to the park can also learn about how being in North Dakota changed how Roosevelt felt about **conservation**. As president, he would work to keep wildlife and public lands safe for the future.

Here, two wild horses walk through tall grass in Theodore Roosevelt National Park. Wild horses have lived in the North Dakota badlands since the nineteenth century.

What's for Dinner?

Because **immigrants** from so many different places settled in North Dakota, the state has many different kinds of food. German settlers brought *fleischkuekle*, a meat pie made with flat bread, and kuchen, a kind of cake. Immigrants from Norway made lutefisk, fish soaked in lye, and *lefse*, a kind of flat bread.

At the Norsk Høstfest, held every fall in Minot, North Dakota, you can try many Scandinavian foods. At the En To Tre buffet, you can eat smoked salmon, lingonberries, and *geitost* cheese. Ready for dessert? Try *tilsorte bondepiker*, which is made with apples, breadcrumbs, and cream. You can also listen to **traditional** Scandinavian music, watch dancers, and meet craftspeople.

At the Norsk Høstfest, you can see people dressed in traditional Scandinavian clothing. These children are wearing traditional Norwegian clothing.

Come to North Dakota!

Whether you like stories of the pioneer days or looking for fossils in the badlands, North Dakota has something for you. In Jamestown, you can see a 60-ton (54 t) statue of a bison or watch a rodeo during Mandan Rodeo Days. At the Lewis and Clark Interpretive Center, you can try on a buffalo coat or sit in a dugout boat.

You can see all kinds of animals at the Dakota Zoo, in Bismarck. You can even stand in Rugby, North Dakota, at the point that marks the exact **geographic** center of North America! Whether you are learning about dinosaurs at the Dakota Dinosaur Museum or seeing the ancient Native American drawings on Writing Rock, you will not be bored in North Dakota!

Glossary

burrows (BUR-ohz) Holes dug in the ground by small animals.

canyons (KAN-yunz) Deep, narrow valleys.

conservation (kon-sur-VAY-shun) Keeping something safe.

economy (ih-KAH-nuh-mee) The way in which a government oversees its supplies, goods, and services.

explorers (ek-SPLOR-erz) People who travel and look for new land.

fossils (FO-sulz) The hardened remains of dead animals or plants.

geographic (jee-uh-GRA-fik) Having to do with the natural features of a place.

immigrants (IH-muh-grunts) People who move to a new country from another country.

petrified (PEH-trih-fyd) Changed into stone.

pioneers (py-uh-NEERZ) Some of the first people to settle in a new area.

refineries (rih-FY-neh-reez) Factories that remove unwanted matter from raw materials like oil or sugar.

Scandinavian (skan-dih-NAY-vee-un) Coming from northern Europe, usually Norway, Sweden, or Denmark.

traditional (truh-DIH-shuh-nul) Done in a way that has been passed down over time.

turbines (TER-bynz) Machines make power by turning the blades or vanes of a spinning wheel, like a windmill.

North Dakota State Symbols

State Tree
American Elm

State Fish
Northern Pike

State Flag

State Bird
Western
Meadowlark

State Flower
Wild Prairie
Rose

State Seal

Famous People from North Dakota

Peggy Lee
(1920–2002)
Born in Jamestown, ND
Jazz Singer

Josh Duhamel
(1972–)
Born in Minot, ND
Actor

Kellan Lutz
(1985–)
Born in Dickinson, ND
Actor/Model

North Dakota State Map

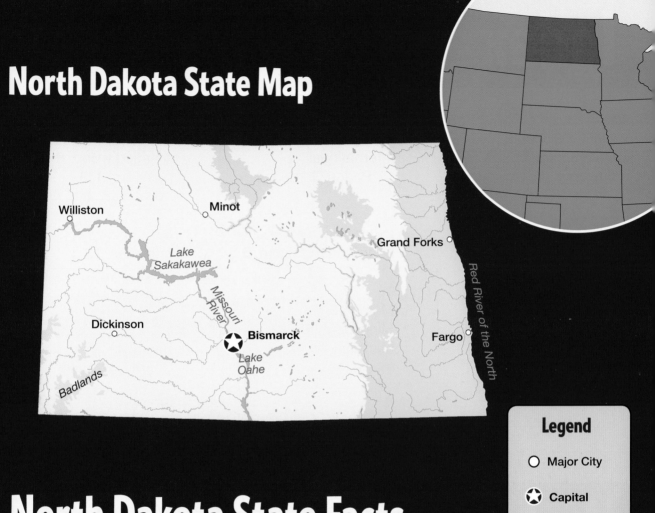

Williston

Minot

Grand Forks

Lake Sakakawea

Missouri River

Dickinson

Bismarck

Lake Oahe

Fargo

Badlands

Red River of the North

Legend

○ Major City

⊛ Capital

〜 *River*

North Dakota State Facts

Population: About 642,200

Area: 70,704 square miles (183,123 sq km)

Motto: "Liberty and Union, Now and Forever, One and Inseparable"

Song: "North Dakota Hymn," words by James Foley and music by
   C. S. Putnam

Index

Web Sites

Due to the changing nature of Internet links, PowerKids Press has developed an online list of Web sites related to the subject of this book. This site is updated regularly. Please use this link to access the list:
www.powerkidslinks.com/amst/nd/